D0190429

JUICES & SMOOTHIES

This book was published in 2015 for Lakeland by Hamlyn, a division of Octopus Publishing Group Limited

Carmelite House
50 Victoria Embankment
London EC4Y 0DZ
United Kingdom
phone +44 (0) 20 3122 6000
www.octopusbooks.co.uk

Printed and bound in China

A catalogue record for this book is available from the British Library.

ISBN 978-0-600-63364-8

Some of the recipes in this book have appeared in other publications.

JUICES & SMOOTHIES

Juices and smoothies are a delicious way to add extra nutrients and vitamins to your diet. From sweet berries and refreshing citrus to crisp vegetables and fresh herbs, this book has over 100 recipes packed full of good-for-you ingredients.

So, whether you want to kickstart your day, have a quick and satisfying snack, encourage your children to enjoy more veg or simply quench your thirst, there's a recipe here for you.

This excellent cookbook is sure to be one of the best-loved on your kitchen bookshelf. To discover the rest of our range of cookbooks, together with our unrivalled selection of creative kitchenware, visit one of our friendly Lakeland stores or shop online at www.lakeland.co.uk.

Contents

Introduction

We all know that fruit and vegetables are key to a healthy, balanced diet, but many of us find it challenging to eat the recommended five portions a day, which is where juices and smoothies come in.

Juicing several types of fruit and vegetables is a quick and easy – not to mention tasty – way to help ensure that you get your full daily nutritional quota.

WHY MAKE YOUR OWN?

So what's the difference between making your own juice or smoothie or buying a carton? The most obvious difference is there are far more nutrients in a fresh, homemade drink than in anything you can buy. Also, bought juices and smoothies are sometimes diluted with water or have additives and preservatives. If you've made it at home yourself, then you know exactly what is in it.

CHOOSING INGREDIENTS

The quality of a juice or smoothie is directly related to the ingredients. For maximum nutrition, try to use the best you can get, choosing those with good colour and optimum ripeness. Organic produce is free from chemical residues, but it is more expensive.

Although fresh is usually best, if fruit and vegetables are frozen soon after picking, they are an excellent option for juices and smoothies. Fruit such as blueberries and raspberries are a good example. If you use canned fruit, make sure it is in natural juice or water, not syrup. Dried fruit, including apricots, prunes and dates, are also a good addition to juices and smoothies.

PREPARATION

Assemble your ingredients but prepare them only just before using them so that fewer nutrients are lost through oxidization and to avoid discoloration.

Wash or scrub all fruit and vegetables that you are not peeling. Always peel avocados, bananas, mangoes, papaya and pineapples but only peel any other ingredients, including vegetables such as carrots or parsnips, if absolutely necessary.

You can leave the skin on unwaxed citrus fruit and on kiwifruit but it is more common to peel them. Remove all stems and large stones from fruit.

For maximum benefit, as ingredients begin to lose nutrition once juiced, aim to drink your juice or smoothie right after you've made it. Store any leftovers in the fridge and consume within 24 hours.

TOP FRUIT AND VEG CHOICES

Most fruit and vegetables can be juiced – experiment with what's in the fridge or fruit bowl to find your own personal favourite combinations and flavours – but there are some ingredients that work particularly well in juices and smoothies.

Apples

Apples are full of antioxidants and also have a naturally sweet flavour that complements sour and savoury ingredients really well. Use apples unpeeled or juice them whole, including the pips, to gain the maximum health benefit.

Apricots

Fresh, dried and canned apricots can be used in juices and smoothies. They have a high beta-carotene and vitamin A content and dried apricots are a good source of iron.

Avocados

Creamy avocados are full of protein and rich in vitamin E. They are best eaten as soon as they are ripe as they start to lose their important antioxidants as they ripen. Cut them and remove the skin and stones at the very last minute to avoid discoloration.

Bananas

Full of carbohydrates for an energy boost, bananas are especially useful in smoothies because they help create a thick, smooth texture.

Beetroot

Beetroot is a great source of folic acid and fibre. It has a sweet taste and makes a tangy and colourful combination with citrus fruit and combines well with berries too.

Blackberries

Rich in vitamin C and full of antioxidants, blackberries mix brilliantly with apples and have a flavour that many children love. The fresh fruit freezes well and can be added to smoothies all year round.

Broccoli

Cheap and available all year round, broccoli is a member of the cruciferous family and is packed with antioxidants and vitamin C. It works well with very sweet fruit, such as pineapple.

Carrots

Delicious in all-veg juices and mixed with fruit, carrots are full of beta-carotene and alpha-carotene and, because of their fibre content, are a good aid to digestion.

Celery

This is a great cleanser and is rich in potassium and phyto-nutrients. It is more easily digested as juice and a few sticks will produce a good yield of juice.

BE CREATIVE

The wider the variety of ingredients you use, the more nutrients your body is getting, so avoid drinking the same juice or smoothie every day. Once you've tried some the recipes in this book, why not have a go at some of your own? Here are a few guidelines to help you come up with your own custom-made recipes:

- Apples and carrots blend well with almost anything
- Bananas and yogurt are ideal as the basis for smoothies
- Avoid too many strong-tasting vegetables in one juice
- If using strong- or bitter-tasting vegetables, dilute and sweeten them with carrot or cucumber
- Taste as you go and adjust the flavouring if it needs it. A squeeze of lemon juice or an extra chunk of apple can make all the difference.

Cranberries

Packed with vitamin C and potassium, these add a distinctive bittersweet flavour and vibrant colour to juices. Children tend to find them too sour, so combine with sweeter fruit and vegetables for child-friendly juices.

Cucumber
Low calorie and hydrating, cucumber is a good base for refreshing juices and smoothies. It is naturally diuretic and contains compounds essential for healthy hair and skin.

Ginger
Adding zip and warmth to juices, among other benefits, ginger is renowned as an immunity booster and is useful against nausea. It partners especially well with lime, lemon, apple, pear, carrot and spinach.

Grapes
Whether green or red, grapes are intensely sweet, so will take the edge off slightly bitter vegetables. They contain potassium and also have a high glucose content, for flagging energy levels.

Kiwifruit
These are full of fibre, vitamin C and potassium. They combine well with all vegetables and fruit and are especially good combined with apples.

Lettuce
This is quite mild tasting so is a good ingredient to add to children's juices. It is rich in beta-carotene, folate and potassium.

Mangoes
A mango will add an exotic flavour to a juice or smoothie and also contains high levels of vitamins A and C.

Oranges and other citrus fruit
Versatile and full of flavour, these are one of the best sources of vitamin C and among the most popular additions to juices and smoothies. To increase the vitamin content of your drink, remove the skin but leave some of the pith attached to the segments.

Peaches
Peaches are good source of vitamin C and antioxidants and excellent for calming an irritated stomach. They make a great addition to summer juices and smoothies.

Pears
Pears are delicious in juices, combining well with other fruit and with vegetables. They are full of vitamin C, potassium and beta-carotene. Make sure you keep the skin on as this contains roughly half of a pear's dietary fibre.

Pineapples
Pineapples contain the digestive enzyme bromelian which is essential in the digestion of protein. They are also rich in vitamin C, potassium and beta-carotene.

Raspberries
Raspberries add great colour and tangy flavour to juices and smoothies and contain magnesium, potassium and vitamin C.

Spinach
Like all leafy greens, this should be a key part of everyone's diet. It is rich in iron and beta-carotene and, although it may seem to some a strange ingredient in a juice, it is well worth trying, either with other vegetables or sweet fruit.

Strawberries
A popular choice in juices and smoothies for both adults and children, strawberries are a good source of vitamin C, calcium and potassium. To make the most of them, freeze them when they are cheap and plentiful in season, then add them to smoothies all year round.

Tomatoes
Adding tomatoes to savoury juices boosts the nutrition count and makes them beautifully colourful. Tomatoes are a good source of vitamin C, fibre and the antioxidant lycopene.

Watermelons
Yielding large amounts of juice, watermelons are a great antioxidant and diuretic fruit. They are also a firm favourite with children because of their mild, sweet taste.

Yogurt
Yogurt is a valuable source of calcium and vitamin D and a key ingredient in many smoothies.

Fruit juices

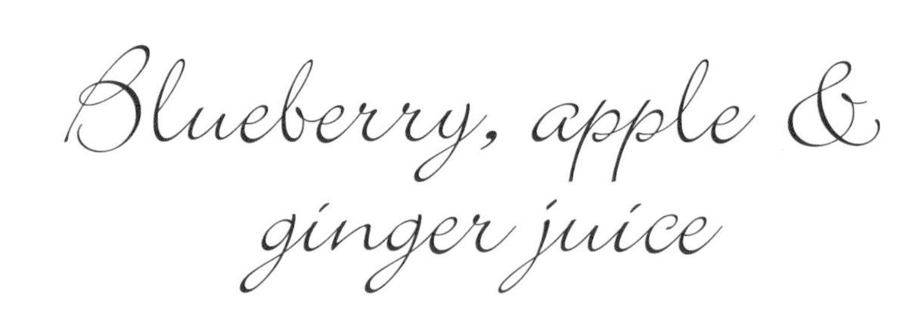

Blueberry, apple & ginger juice

2.5 cm piece fresh root ginger, roughly chopped, plus extra to serve (optional)
250 g blueberries
125 g grapefruit
250 g apples
ice cubes (optional)

1 Peel and roughly chop the ginger. Juice the blueberries, grapefruit and apple with the ginger.
2 Pour the juice into a glass over ice, if using, decorate with thin slices of ginger, if liked, and serve immediately.

makes about 200 ml
tip For apple & ginger juice, juice 250 g apple with 2.5 cm ginger. If you like, top it up with ice-cold water.

Watermelon & raspberry juice

300 g watermelon
125 g raspberries
crushed ice (optional)

1 Peel the melon as close to the skin as possible and roughly chop.
2 Juice the watermelon and raspberries, then press the juice through a sieve over a bowl to remove any raspberry pips.
3 Pour the juice into glasses over some crushed ice, if liked.

makes about 200 ml

Strawberry, redcurrant & orange juice

100 g strawberries
75 g redcurrants, plus extra to serve (optional)
½ orange, about 100 g
125 ml still water
½ teaspoon clear honey (optional)
ice cubes

1 Hull the strawberries. Remove the stalks from the redcurrants and peel and segment the orange. Juice the fruit, add the water and stir in the honey, if using.
2 Pour the juice into a glass, add some ice cubes and decorate with extra redcurrants, if liked.

makes about 225 ml

Papaya, raspberry & grapefruit juice

150 g papaya
150 g grapefruit
150 g raspberries
juice of ½ lime, plus slices to serve (optional)
2–3 ice cubes (optional)

1 Deseed papaya and scoop out the flesh. Segment the grapefruit, leaving the pith on, and juice it with the papaya and raspberries and lime juice.
2 Pour into a glass, add the ice cubes, if using, and decorate with lime slices if liked.

makes about 200 ml

Grape & plum juice

300 g plums, plus extra to serve (optional)
150 g red grapes
2–3 crushed ice cubes

1 Remove the stones from the plums then cut the flesh into even-sized pieces. Juice with the grapes.
2 Pour the juice into a tall glass, add a couple of crushed ice cubes, decorate with slices of plum, if liked, and serve immediately.

makes about 300 ml

Apple, mango & passionfruit juice

1 mango, about 200 g
2 passionfruit
3 red apples, about 300 g in total
ice cubes

1 Peel the mango and remove the stone. Slice the passionfruit in half and scoop out the pulp. Juice the apples with mango and passionfruit pulp.
2 Pour the juice into a tall glass over ice and serve immediately.

makes about 300 ml

Orange & raspberry juice

2 large oranges, about 400 g in total
175 g raspberries
250 ml water
ice cubes (optional)

1 Roughly peel the oranges. Juice the oranges with the raspberries then add the water.
2 Pour the juice into 2 tall glasses over ice, if using, and serve immediately.

makes about 500 ml

Apple, apricot & peach juice

3 apricots, about 225 g in total
1 peach, 125 g, plus extra to serve (optional)
2 apples, about 200 g in total
ice cubes

1 Halve and stone the apricots and peach. Juice the apples with the apricots and peach.
2 Transfer the juice to a food processor or blender, add a few ice cubes and process for 10 seconds.
3 Pour the juice into a glass, decorate with peach slices, if liked, and serve immediately.

makes about 200 ml

Peachy plum juice

4 plums, about 300 g in total
3 peaches, about 450 g in total
2 apricots, about 150 g in total
1 carrot, about 150 g
ice cubes

1 Remove the stones from the plums, peaches and apricots. Juice all the ingredients together.
2 Pour the juice into a glass over ice and serve immediately.

makes about 200 ml
tip For gingered plum juice, stone 4 plums – about 300 g in total. Juice the plums with 2 carrots – about 300 g in total – and a 2 cm piece peeled fresh root ginger. Stir in a large pinch of grated nutmeg and serve.

Orange & passionfruit sparkler

100 g orange
1 passionfruit
100 ml sparkling mineral water
2–3 ice cubes

1 Peel, segment and juice the orange. Scoop the flesh out of the passionfruit and press the pulp through a sieve to extract the juice.
2 Mix the orange juice with the passionfruit juice and sparkling water. Pour into a glass over ice and serve immediately.

makes about 200 ml

Peach & ginger juice

250 g peaches
2.5 cm piece fresh root ginger, roughly chopped
ice cubes
sparkling mineral water
mint leaves, to serve

1 Halve the peaches and remove the stones. Peel and roughly chop the ginger. Juice the peach with the ginger.
2 Pour the juice into a tall glass over ice, add a splash of sparkling mineral water and a couple of mint leaves and serve immediately.

makes about 200 ml

Dried apricot & pineapple juice

65 g ready-to-eat dried apricots
350 ml pineapple juice
2–3 ice cubes

1 Roughly chop the dried apricots and put them into a large bowl. Pour over the pineapple juice, cover and leave to stand overnight in the refrigerator.
2 Transfer the apricots and juice to a food processor or blender and process until thick and smooth.
3 Pour the juice into a tall glass, add a couple of ice cubes and serve immediately.

makes about 350 ml

Pear & pineapple juice

200 g pineapple or canned pineapple
in its own juices
½ lemon
2 pears, about 450 g in total
ice cubes

1 Peel and core the pineapple. Peel the lemon and juice with the pineapple and pears.
2 Pour into a glass over ice and serve immediately.

makes about 200 ml

Apple, pineapple & melon juice

½ galia melon, about 500 g
¼ pineapple, about 250 g
3 green apples, about 300 g in total
ice cubes (optional)

1 Peel and deseed the melon. Peel and core the pineapple. Chop all the fruit into even-sized pieces and juice.
2 Pour the juice into a glass over ice, if using, and serve immediately.

makes about 200 ml

Pear, kiwifruit & lime juice

3 kiwifruit, about 225 g in total, plus extra to serve
½ lime
2 pears, about 350 g in total
2–3 ice cubes (optional)

1 Peel the kiwifruit and lime and juice with the pears.
2 Pour into a tall glass, add the ice cubes, if using, decorate with slices of kiwifruit and serve immediately.

makes about 300 ml

Great grapefruit juice

2 grapefruit, about 300 g
1 kiwifruit, about 75 g
1 apple, about 100 g, plus extra to serve
½ cucumber, about 175 g

1 Roughly peel the grapefruit and kiwifruit. Juice all the ingredients together.
2 Pour the juice into a glass, decorate with a slice of apple and serve immediately.

makes about 350 ml

Mango & melon juice

1 mango, about 200 g
½ galia melon, about 500 g
200 ml orange juice
ice cubes

1 Peel the mango, remove the stone and roughly chop the flesh. Peel and deseed the galia melon and roughly chop the flesh.
2 Juice the fruit. Transfer to a food processor or blender, add the orange juice and a couple of ice cubes and process until smooth.
3 Pour the juice into 2 glasses and serve immediately.

makes about 400 ml

Kiwi sparkler

3 kiwifruit, about 225 g in total
2 cm piece fresh root ginger
1 apple, about 100 g
ice cubes (optional)
300 ml sparkling water

1 Peel the kiwifruit and ginger. Juice the kiwifruit with the ginger and apple.
2 Pour the juice into a glass over ice, if liked, top up with sparkling water and serve immediately.

makes about 300 ml

Cool currants juice

2 apples, about 200 g in total
300 g blackcurrants
100 g redcurrants
sprig of blackcurrants or redcurrants, to serve

1 Juice all the ingredients together.
2 Pour the juice into a glass, decorate with a sprig of currants and serve immediately.

makes about 300 ml

Forest fruits juice

200 g blackberries
100 g blueberries
1 apple, about 100 g

1 Juice all the ingredients together.
2 Pour the juice into a glass and serve immediately.

makes about 300 ml
tip For green forest fruits juice, juice 1 apple – about 100 g – with 200 g blackberries, 30 g kale and a 2 cm piece peeled fresh root ginger.

Blackberry, melon & kiwi juice

100 g cantaloupe melon
2 kiwifruit, about 150 g
100 g fresh or frozen blackberries, thawed, plus extra to serve
2–3 ice cubes

1 Peel the melon as close to the skin as possible. Roughly peel the kiwifruit. Juice the melon with the kiwifruit and blackberries.
2 Transfer the juice to a food processor or blender and process with a couple of ice cubes.
3 Pour into a glass and decorate with a few blackberries.

makes about 250 ml

Pear & cranberry juice

1 large pear, about 175 g
100 ml cranberry juice
ice cubes

1 Juice the pear. Mix the pear juice with the cranberry juice.
2 Pour the combined juices into a glass over ice and serve immediately.

makes about 200 ml
tip For cranberry & cucumber juice, use the same amount of cranberry juice and add the juice of 1 orange and 50 g cucumber.

Vegetable juices

Carrot & kiwi juice

1 kiwifruit, plus extra to serve (optional)
200 g carrot
ice cubes (optional)

1 Roughly peel the kiwifruit. Cut the carrot and kiwifruit into even-sized pieces and juice together.
2 Pour the juice into a glass over ice, if using, decorate with slices of kiwifruit, if liked, and serve immediately.

makes about 250 ml
tip For cucumber & kiwifruit juice, omit the carrots and instead juice 1½ cucumbers with the kiwifruit. Serve with a squeeze of lemon.

Orange, beet & apple juice

1 orange, about 160 g
1 beetroot, about 125 g
1 apple, about 125 g
ice cubes

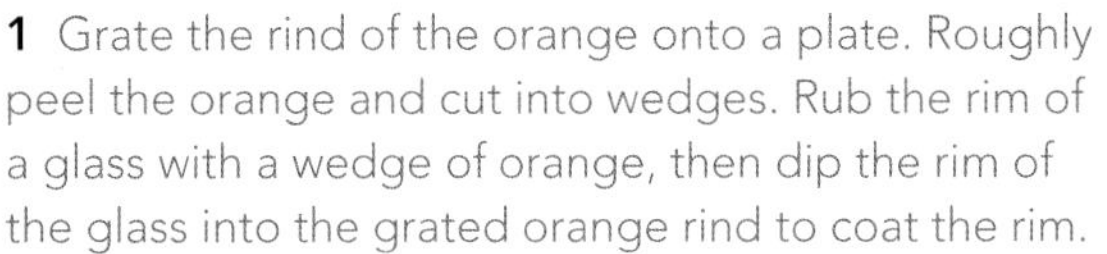

1 Grate the rind of the orange onto a plate. Roughly peel the orange and cut into wedges. Rub the rim of a glass with a wedge of orange, then dip the rim of the glass into the grated orange rind to coat the rim.
2 Juice together the orange wedges, beetroot and apple.
3 Pour the juice into the prepared glass over ice and serve immediately.

makes about 350 ml

Citrus beet juice

1 orange, about 160 g
1 beetroot, about 125 g
1 carrot, about 150 g, plus extra to serve
½ cucumber, about 175 g

1 Roughly peel the orange. Juice the orange with the beetroot, carrot and cucumber.
2 Pour the juice into a glass, decorate with slices of carrot and serve immediately.

makes about 400 ml

Spinach power juice

60 g spinach
2 celery sticks
1 apple, about 100 g

1 Juice all the ingredients together.
2 Pour the juice into a glass and serve immediately.

makes about 250 ml

Parsnip, pepper & watercress juice

175 g green pepper
100 g watercress
175 g cucumber
175 g parsnip
ice cubes
mint sprigs, to serve

1 Core and deseed the pepper. Juice the watercress and cucumber with the parsnip and peppers.
2 Pour the juice into a glass over ice, decorate with mint sprigs and serve immediately.

makes about 200 ml

Lettuce, grape & ginger juice

2.5 cm piece fresh root ginger, chopped
200 g green grapes, plus extra to serve (optional)
200 g lettuce
ice cubes (optional)

1 Peel and roughly chop the ginger. Juice the grapes and lettuce with the ginger.
2 Pour the juice into a glass, decorate with a few grapes, if liked, and serve immediately.

makes about 200 ml

Fabulous fennel juice

1 fennel bulb, about 150 g
1 apple, about 100 g
1 carrot, about 150 g
grated nutmeg, to serve

1 Juice all the ingredients together.
2 Pour the juice into a glass, sprinkle with a large pinch of nutmeg and serve immediately.

makes about 300 ml

Blueberry, cucumber & apple juice

300 g blueberries
½ cucumber, about 175 g
1 apple, about 100 g

1 Juice all the ingredients together.
2 Pour the juice into a glass and serve immediately.

makes about 300 ml

Blackberry, apple & celeriac juice

100 g celeriac
50 g apple
100 g frozen blackberries, plus extra to serve
2–3 ice cubes

1 Peel the celeriac. Juice the celeriac with the apple.
2 Transfer the juice to a food processor or blender, add the blackberries and the ice cubes and process briefly.
3 Pour the juice into a glass, decorate with extra blackberries and serve immediately.

makes about 200 ml

Minty summer vegetable juice

6 asparagus spears
½ cucumber, about 175 g
2 young carrots, about 200 g
small handful of mint, plus an extra mint sprig to serve
ice cubes

1 Juice together the asparagus, cucumber, carrots and mint.
2 Pour the juice into a glass over ice, top with a sprig of mint and serve immediately.

makes about 300 ml

Cabbage, apple & cinnamon juice

200 g green cabbage
50 g apple
2–3 ice cubes
ground cinnamon, plus extra to serve

1 Separate the cabbage into leaves and cut the apple into pieces. Juice the cabbage with the apple.
2 Transfer the juice to a food processor or blender, add a couple of ice cubes and a sprinkling of cinnamon and process briefly.
3 Pour the juice into a glass, decorate with a sprinkling of cinnamon and serve immediately.

makes about 200 ml

Fennel & camomile juice

1 lemon, plus extra to serve
150 g fennel bulb
100 ml chilled camomile tea
ice cubes

1 Roughly peel the lemon and juice it with the fennel. Mix the juice with the chilled camomile tea.
2 Pour the combined juice and tea into a glass over ice and serve with slices of lemon.

makes about 200 ml

Celeriac, alfalfa & orange juice

100 g orange, plus extra to serve (optional)
100 g celeriac
100 g alfalfa sprouts

1 Peel the orange and separate it into segments. Peel the celeriac and cut it into chunks. Rinse the alfalfa sprouts. Juice the ingredients.
2 Pour the juice into a glass, add slices of orange, if liked, and serve immediately.

makes about 200 ml

Tomato, red pepper & papaya juice

125 g papaya
100 g red pepper
1 large tomato, about 125 g
2–3 ice cubes

1 Peel and deseed the papaya. Core and deseed the pepper. Juice the tomato with the papaya and pepper.
2 Transfer the juice to a food processor or blender, add a couple of ice cubes and process.
3 Pour the juice into a glass and serve immediately.

makes about 200 ml

Tomato, apple & basil juice

1 celery stick
4 large tomatoes, about 400 g in total
1 apple
ice cubes
4 basil leaves, finely chopped, plus extra to serve (optional)
1½ tablespoons lime juice

1 Trim the celery and cut it into 5 cm lengths. Juice the tomatoes and apple with the celery.
2 Pour the juice into a glass over ice, stir in the basil leaves and lime juice, decorate with extra chopped basil, if liked, and serve immediately.

makes about 200 ml
tip For tomato, cauliflower & carrot juice, trim 100 g cauliflower and juice with 1 large tomato and 200 g carrot.

Broccoli, parsnip & apple juice

50 g parsnip
50 g apple
150 g broccoli
2–3 ice cubes

1 Peel the parsnip and cut the flesh into chunks. Quarter the apple and trim the broccoli. Juice the parsnip with the apple and broccoli.
2 Transfer the juice to a food processor or blender and process with the ice cubes.
3 Pour into a glass and serve immediately.

makes about 200 ml

Carrot, radish & cucumber juice

100 g potato
100 g radish, plus extra to serve (optional)
100 g carrot
100 g cucumber
ice cubes

1 Juice the potato, radish, carrot and cucumber.
2 Transfer the juice to a food processor or blender, add a couple of ice cubes and process briefly.
3 Pour the juice into a glass over ice, decorate with slices of radish, if liked, and serve immediately.

makes about 200 ml
tip For carrot, radish & ginger juice, omit the potato and cucumber and add 2.5 cm peeled and roughly chopped fresh root ginger. This is a good juice if you have a cold or blocked sinuses.

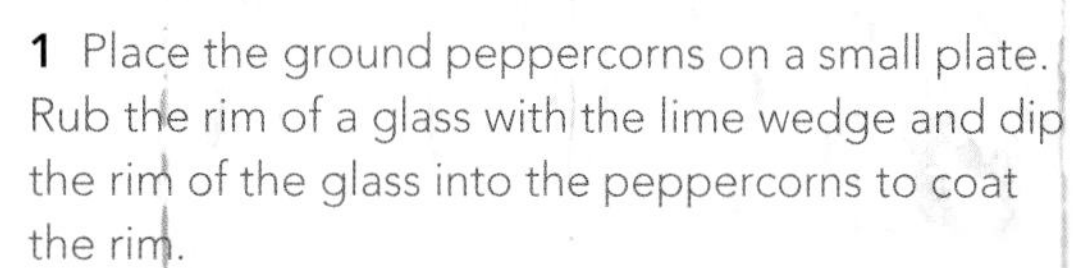

Sweet pepper juice

1 teaspoon ground mixed peppercorns
lime wedge
1 red pepper, about 175 g
20 red grapes
2–3 ice cubes

1 Place the ground peppercorns on a small plate. Rub the rim of a glass with the lime wedge and dip the rim of the glass into the peppercorns to coat the rim.
2 Core and deseed the red pepper. Juice the pepper with the grapes.
3 Transfer the juice to a food processor or blender, add the ice cubes and process briefly until smooth.
4 Pour the juice into the prepared glass and serve immediately.

makes about 250 ml

Salad in a glass

1 celery stick
¼ cucumber, about 65 g
2 tomatoes, about 200 g in total
2 Little Gem lettuces, about 275 g in total
2 carrots, about 300 g in total
1 apple, about 100 g
ice cubes

1 Juice together the celery, cucumber, tomatoes, lettuce, carrots and apple.
2 Pour the juice into a glass over ice and serve immediately.

makes about 300 ml

Spicy beetroot juice

1 large beetroot, about 175 g
15 g coriander leaves
2 celery sticks
large pinch of ground turmeric
pepper

1 Juice the beetroot with the coriander and celery. Whisk in the ground turmeric. Season the juice to taste with pepper.
2 Pour the juice into a glass and serve immediately.

makes about 250 ml

Purple power juice

2 cm piece fresh root ginger
100 g red cabbage
1 celery stick
1 apple, about 100 g
12 red grapes
ice cubes

1 Peel the ginger. Juice together the peeled ginger, cabbage, celery, apple and grapes.
2 Pour the juice into a glass over ice and serve immediately.

makes about 300 ml

Carrot, chilli & pineapple juice

½ small chilli
250 g pineapple
250 g carrot
ice cubes
juice of ½ lime
1 tablespoon chopped coriander leaves

1 Deseed the chilli. Remove the core and peel from the pineapple. Juice the carrots with the chilli and pineapple.
2 Pour the juice into a glass over ice. Squeeze over the lime juice, stir in the chopped coriander and serve immediately.

makes about 200 ml

Beautiful brussels juice

2 cm piece fresh root ginger
6 Brussels sprouts
1 carrot, about 150 g
1 apple, about 100 g

1 Peel the ginger. Juice all the ingredients together.
2 Pour the juice into a glass and serve immediately.

makes about 300 ml
tip For bountiful Brussels juice, juice 10 Brussels sprouts with 2 celery sticks, 1 carrot – about 150 g, 100 g broccoli and 1 apple – about 100 g.

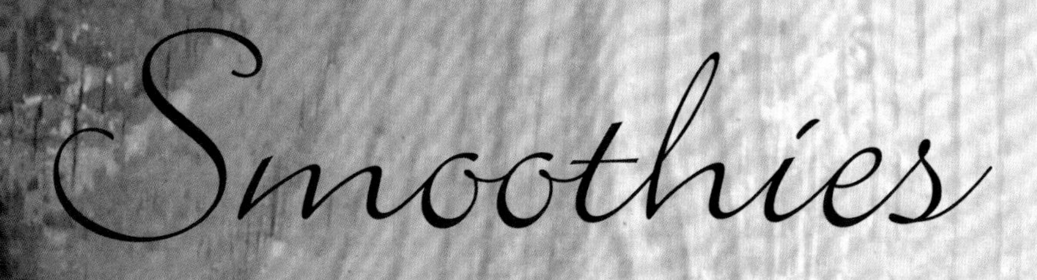

Smoothies

Perfect passion smoothie

1 lime
2 large mangoes, about 1.15 kg
5 passionfruit
225 g natural yogurt
2 handfuls ice cubes

1 Roughly peel and then juice the lime. Peel and stone the mangoes.
2 Transfer the lime juice and mangoes to a food processor or blender. Halve the passionfruit, scoop out the pulp and add all but 1 tablespoon to the blender with the yogurt and ice cubes and process until smooth.
3 Pour the smoothie into glasses, decorate with the remaining passionfruit pulp and serve immediately.

makes about 750 ml

Tropical fruit smoothie

1 large banana, about 200 g
1 large ripe mango, about 500g
150 g natural yogurt
300 ml pineapple juice
pineapple chunks, to serve (optional)

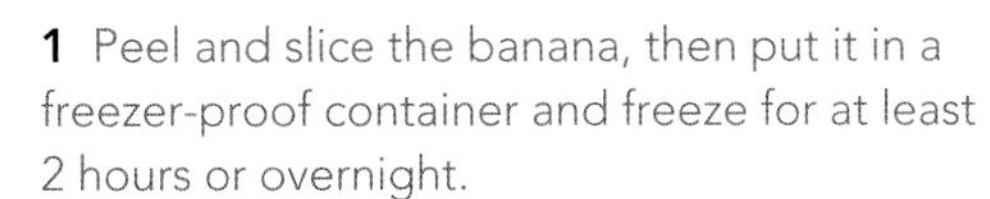

1 Peel and slice the banana, then put it in a freezer-proof container and freeze for at least 2 hours or overnight.
2 Peel the mango, remove the stone and roughly chop the flesh. Place the flesh in a food processor or blender with the frozen banana, yogurt and pineapple juice and process until smooth.
3 Pour the mixture into glasses, decorate with pineapple chunks, if liked, and serve immediately.

makes about 600 ml

Banana & maple syrup smoothie

2 bananas, about 350 g in total
300 ml milk
4 tablespoons natural fromage frais
3 tablespoons maple syrup
50 g hot oat cereal

To serve
banana slices
malt loaf chunks

1 Peel and chop the bananas.
2 Place the bananas in a food processor or blender with the milk, fromage frais and maple syrup and process until smooth. Add the oat cereal and process again to thicken.
3 Pour into 2 glasses. Arrange banana slices and chunks of malt loaf on 2 cocktail sticks and balance them across the top of the glasses, to decorate.

makes about 400 ml

Cherry & chocolate smoothie

100 g blueberries
200 g cherries
1 tablespoon cocoa nibs, plus extra to serve
300 ml milk

1 Juice the blueberries. Stone the cherries.
2 Transfer the blueberry juice and cherries to a food processor or blender, add the cocoa nibs and milk and process until smooth.
3 Pour the smoothie into glasses, sprinkle with some extra cocoa nibs and serve immediately.

makes about 250 ml

Dried fruit & apple smoothie

125 g dried fruit salad
about 400 ml apple juice
200 ml Greek yogurt
ice cubes (optional)

1 Roughly chop the dried fruit salad and place it in a large bowl. Pour over the apple juice, cover the bowl and leave to stand overnight.
2 Put the dried fruit and apple juice in a food processor or blender, add the yogurt and process until smooth, adding a little more apple juice if necessary.
3 Pour the smoothie into glasses, add a couple of ice cubes, if using, and serve immediately.

makes about 450 ml

Cranberry & apple smoothie

250 g apple
100 g frozen cranberries
100 g natural yogurt
1 tablespoon clear honey
ice cubes (optional)

1 Juice the apples.
2 Transfer the juice to a food processor or blender, add the cranberries, yogurt and honey and process briefly.
3 Pour the smoothie into a glass over ice, if using, and serve immediately.

makes about 200 ml

Strawberry beet smoothie

50 g beetroot
100 g blueberries
100 g strawberries, plus extra to serve
2–3 ice cubes

1 Juice the beetroot.
2 Pour the beetroot juice into a food processor or blender, add the blueberries, strawberries and ice cubes and process until smooth.
3 Pour the mixture into a glass, decorate with strawberries, if liked, and serve immediately.

makes about 250 ml

Banana, orange & mango smoothie

1 banana, about 175 g
1 mango, about 200 g
200 ml orange juice
200 ml semi-skimmed milk
3 tablespoons natural fromage frais
ice cubes (optional)

1 Peel and slice the banana. Peel the mango, remove the stone and cut the flesh into even-sized pieces.
2 Put the banana and mango in a food processor or blender, add the orange juice, milk and fromage frais and process until smooth.
3 Pour the smoothie into glasses over ice, if using, and serve immediately.

makes about 500 ml

Mango & passionfruit smoothie

1 large mango, about 200 g
750 g natural yogurt
1–2 tablespoons agave nectar, to taste
1 vanilla pod, split in half lengthways
4 passionfruit, halved
biscuits to serve (optional)

1 Stone and peel the mango.
2 Transfer the mango to a food processor or blender and process to a purée.
3 Put the yogurt and agave nectar, according to taste, in a large bowl, scrape in the seeds from the vanilla pod and beat together. Gently fold in the mango purée and spoon into tall glasses.
4 Scoop the pulp from the passionfruit and spoon over the smoothie. Serve immediately with thin biscuits, if liked.

makes about 750 ml

Breakfast smoothie

2 large oranges, about 400 g in total
1 banana, about 175 g
2 tablespoons muesli
300 ml milk
ground cinnamon, to serve

1 Roughly peel and juice the oranges. Peel the banana.
2 Transfer the orange juice and banana to a food processor or blender, add the muesli and milk and process until smooth.
3 Pour the smoothie into glasses, sprinkle with ground cinnamon and serve immediately.

makes about 400 ml

Cucumber lassi

150 g cucumber
150 g natural yogurt
100 ml ice-cold water
handful of mint
½ teaspoon ground cumin
squeeze of lemon juice

1 Peel and roughly chop the cucumber. Place in a food processor or blender and add the yogurt and water.
2 Pull the mint leaves off their stalks, reserving a few for decoration, if liked. Chop the remainder roughly and put them into the food processor. Add the cumin and lemon juice and process briefly.
3 Pour the smoothie into a glass, decorate with mint leaves, if using, and serve immediately.

makes about 400 ml

Strawberry lassi

400 g strawberries
750 ml ice-cold water
300 ml natural yogurt
25 g golden caster sugar
few drops of rosewater
coarsely ground black pepper, to serve

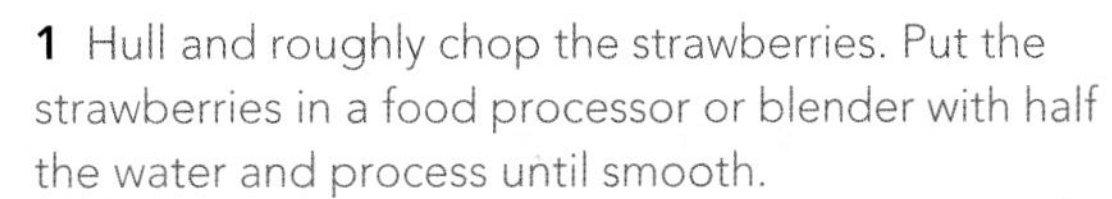

1 Hull and roughly chop the strawberries. Put the strawberries in a food processor or blender with half the water and process until smooth.
2 Add the yogurt, sugar, rosewater and the remaining water and process again until smooth and frothy.
3 Pour the smoothie into glasses, sprinkle with black pepper and serve immediately.

makes about 1.5 litres

Dairy-free smoothies

Summer smoothie

½ lime
small handful mint, plus an extra sprig to serve
125 g gooseberries
30 g ground almonds
150 ml non-dairy milk
1 teaspoon elderflower cordial

1 Roughly peel the lime. Juice the lime with the mint.
2 Transfer the juice to a food processor or blender, add the remaining ingredients and process until smooth.
3 Pour the smoothie into a glass, decorate with a sprig of mint and serve immediately.

makes about 200 ml

Melon, mint & strawberry smoothie

1 kg watermelon
14–16 strawberries
12 mint leaves
small handful of ice cubes

1 Peel the melon as close to the skin as possible. Hull the strawberries.
2 Place all the ingredients in a food processor or blender and process until smooth.
3 Pour into glasses and serve immediately.

makes about 750 ml

Orange, mango & strawberry smoothie

125 g strawberries
1 small mango, about 200 g
300 ml orange juice
orange slices, to serve (optional)

1 Hull the strawberries, put them in a freezer container and freeze for 2 hours or overnight.
2 Peel the mango, remove the stone, roughly chop the flesh and put it in a food processor or blender with the strawberries and orange juice and process until thick.
3 Pour the smoothie into a glass, decorate with slices of orange, if liked, and serve immediately.

makes about 400 ml

Peanut butter & banana smoothie

½ lime
150g banana
1 tablespoon peanut butter
300 ml almond milk
grated nutmeg, to serve

1 Roughly peel and juice the lime. Peel the banana.
2 Transfer the lime juice and banana to a food processor or blender, add the peanut butter and almond milk and process until smooth.
3 Pour the smoothie into glasses, sprinkle with a large pinch of nutmeg and serve immediately.

makes about 400 ml

Strawberry & soya smoothie

100 g fresh or frozen strawberries
2 kiwifruit
200 ml soya milk
ice cubes (optional)
25 g flaked almonds, to serve (optional)

1 Hull the strawberries and peel the kiwifruit. Place in a food processor or blender with the milk and kiwifruit and process briefly. If you are using fresh strawberries add a few ice cubes and process until smooth.
2 Pour the mixture into a glass, decorate with flaked almonds, if liked, and serve immediately.

makes about 250 ml

Mandarin & lychee frappé

100 g mandarin oranges, canned in natural juice
50 g lychees, canned in natural juice
ice cubes

1 Put the oranges and lychees and the juices from the cans into a food processor or blender, add the ice cubes and process briefly.
2 Pour the frappé into a glass and serve immediately.

makes about 150 ml

Cucumber, lemon & mint smoothie

250 g cucumber, plus extra to serve
½ lemon
3–4 fresh mint leaves
2–3 ice cubes

1 Peel and roughly chop the cucumber. Roughly peel the lemon.
2 Put the cucumber and lemon into a food processor or blender with the mint leaves and ice cubes and process briefly.
3 Pour the smoothie into a glass, decorate with a strip of cucumber, if liked, and serve immediately.

makes about 300 ml

Mango, pineapple & lime smoothie

1 mango, about 200 g
300 ml pineapple juice
rind and juice of ½ lime
lime wedges, to serve (optional)

1 Peel the mango, remove the stone, roughly chop the flesh and put it in a freezer container. Freeze for at least 2 hours or overnight.
2 Put the frozen mango in a food processor or blender, add the pineapple juice and lime rind and juice and process until thick.
3 Pour the smoothie into glasses, decorate with lime wedges, if liked, and serve immediately.

makes about 400 ml

Pineapple, parsnip & carrot smoothie

250 g pineapple, plus extra to serve (optional)
100 g parsnip
100 g carrot
75 ml soya milk
ice cubes

1 Peel the pineapple, remove the core and cut the flesh into chunks. Juice the parsnips and carrots with the pineapple.
2 Transfer the juice to a food processor or blender, add the soya milk and some ice cubes and process until smooth.
3 Pour the mixture into glasses, decorate with pineapple wedges, if liked, and serve immediately.

makes about 300 ml

Berry blast smoothie

2 apples, about 200 g
1 large banana, about 200 g
250 g mixed berries (such as blueberries, blackberries, raspberries and strawberries), plus extra to serve
ice cubes

1 Juice the apples. Peel the banana.
2 Transfer the apple juice and banana to a food processor or blender, add the mixed berries and process until smooth, adding a little water, if necessary, if you want a looser consistency.
3 Pour the smoothie into glasses over ice, decorate with a few extra berries and serve immediately.

makes about 350 ml
tip For berry green smoothie, follow the recipe above, adding 60 g spinach to the juicer with the apple.

Blueberry & mint smoothie

100 g frozen blueberries
150 ml soya milk
small bunch of mint

1 Put the blueberries in a food processor or blender and pour in the soya milk. Pull the mint leaves off their stalks, reserving one or two sprigs for decoration, and add the remainder to the blender. Process briefly.
2 Pour the smoothie into glasses, decorate with the reserved mint sprigs and serve immediately.

makes about 200 ml

Prune, apple & cinnamon smoothie

65 g ready-to-eat prunes
pinch of ground cinnamon,
plus extra to serve
350 ml apple juice
3 tablespoons soya yogurt
ice cubes

1 Roughly chop the prunes. Put the prunes and cinnamon in a large bowl, pour over the apple juice, cover and leave to stand overnight.
2 Put the prunes, apple juice and yogurt in a food processor or blender and process until smooth.
3 Pour the smoothie into glasses over ice cubes, sprinkle with extra cinnamon and serve immediately.

makes about 400 ml

Super health boosters

Apple, banana & wheatgerm smoothie

2 tablespoons wheatgerm
1 tablespoon sesame seeds
2 bananas, about 350 g in total
75 g pineapple
450 ml apple juice
300 ml natural yogurt

1 Spread the wheatgerm and sesame seeds over a baking sheet and toast gently under a preheated grill, stirring a couple of times until the sesame seeds have begun to turn a golden brown. Remove from the grill and leave to cool.
2 Peel and slice the bananas. Remove the skin and core from the pineapple and chop the flesh. Put the banana and pineapple in a food processor or blender and process to a rough purée.
3 Add the apple juice and blend again to make a smooth juice. Add the yogurt and the cooled wheatgerm and sesame seeds. Blend again.
4 Pour into glasses and serve immediately.

makes about 1 litre

Kick start juice

1 lemon
2 cm piece fresh root ginger
1 garlic clove
1 apple, about 100 g
1 carrot, about 150 g
2 celery sticks
100 g alfalfa sprouts

1 Roughly peel the lemon, ginger and garlic. Juice all the ingredients together.
2 Pour the juice into a glass and serve immediately.

makes about 350 ml
tip For clean start juice, juice 1 roughly peeled lemon with 1 roughly peeled lime, ½ cucumber – about 175 g – and a 2 cm piece peeled fresh root ginger. Pour the juice into a tall glass and top up with sparkling water.

Exotic elixir

1 orange, about 200 g
1 kiwifruit, about 75 g, plus extra to serve
2 apricots, about 125 g in total
1 slice pineapple, about 180 g
1 carrot, about 150 g

1 Roughly peel the orange and kiwifruit. Remove the stones from the apricots. Remove the skin from the pineapple. Juice all the ingredients together.
2 Pour the juice into a glass, decorate with a slice of kiwifruit and serve immediately.

makes about 300 ml

Red onion & beetroot juice

125 g watercress
125 g red onion
1 garlic clove
250 g carrot
125 g beetroot, plus leaves to serve (optional)

1 Juice the watercress, onion and garlic with the carrot and beetroot.
2 Pour the juice into a glass, decorate with beetroot leaves, if liked, and serve immediately.

makes about 200 ml

Beetroot & berry smoothie

50 g beetroot
100 g blueberries, plus extra to serve (optional)
100 g raspberries
2–3 ice cubes

1 Juice the beetroot. Pour the beetroot juice into a food processor or blender, add the blueberries, raspberries and ice cubes and process until smooth.
2 Pour the mixture into a glass, decorate with blueberries, if liked, and serve immediately.

makes about 250 ml

Five fruits juice

2 clementines, about 200 g in total
6 cherries
1 apricot, about 65 g
1 apple, about 100 g
6 red grapes
1 lemon grass stalk
ice cubes

1 Peel the clementines. Stone the cherries and apricot. Juice together with the apple, grapes and lemon grass.
2 Pour into a glass over ice and serve immediately.

makes about 300 ml

Super fruits juice

1 kiwifruit, about 75 g
25 g fresh or frozen (defrosted) cranberries
50 g pomegranate seeds
100 g blueberries
1 carrot, about 150 g

1 Peel the kiwifruit. Juice all the ingredients together.
2 Pour the juice into a glass and serve immediately.

makes about 300 ml

Seven vegetable juice

50 g green pepper
50 g celery
90 g carrot
25 g spinach
25 g onion
90 g cucumber
50 g tomatoes, plus extra to serve (optional)
sea salt and pepper

1 Core and deseed the pepper. Trim the celery and cut it into 5 cm lengths. Juice the carrot, spinach, onion, cucumber and tomato with the pepper and celery.
2 Pour the juice into a glass and season with sea salt and black pepper. Decorate with tomato quarters, if liked, and serve immediately.

makes about 200 ml

Pomegranate plus juice

1 lemon
2 pomegranates, about 500 g in total
200 g blueberries

1 Roughly peel the lemon. Remove the seeds from the pomegranate by cutting the fruit in half, then holding the halved fruit over a bowl and hitting the skin with a wooden spoon so that the seeds fall into the bowl. Juice all the ingredients together.
2 Pour the juice into a glass and serve immediately.

makes about 250 ml
tip For peachy pomegranate juice, remove the seeds from 1 pomegranate – about 250 g in total. Juice the pomegranate seeds with 2 stoned peaches – about 300 g in total, 1 apple – about 100 g – and 1 carrot – about 150 g

Carrot, beet & sweet potato juice

175 g sweet potato or yam
100 g beetroot
175 g carrot
125 g fennel
ice cubes
fennel fronds, to serve (optional)

1 Peel the sweet potato or yam and juice with the beetroot, carrot and fennel.
2 Pour the juice into a glass over ice, decorate with fennel fronds, if liked, and serve immediately.

makes about 200 ml

Superfood smoothie

25 g cranberries
50 g pomegranate seeds
25 g kale
1 beetroot, about 100 g
1 banana, about 175 g
1 tablespoon goji berries
50 g strawberries
500 ml milk
1 tablespoon avocado oil
1 tablespoon sesame seeds, to serve

1 Juice the cranberries with the pomegranate seeds, kale and beetroot.
2 Transfer the juice to a food processor or blender, add the remaining ingredients and process until smooth.
3 Pour the smoothie into glasses, sprinkle with sesame seeds and serve immediately.

makes about 750 ml

Tomato, carrot & ginger juice

2.5 cm cube fresh root ginger
100 g celery, plus extra to serve (optional)
300 g tomatoes
175 g carrot
1 garlic clove
2.5 cm piece fresh horseradish
2–3 ice cubes

1 Peel and roughly chop the ginger. Trim the celery and cut it into 5 cm lengths. Juice the tomatoes, carrot, garlic and horseradish with the ginger and celery.
2 Transfer the juice to a food processor or blender, add a couple of ice cubes and process briefly.
3 Pour the juice into a glass, garnish with celery slivers, if liked, and serve immediately.

makes about 150 ml

Banana & fig smoothie

2.5 cm piece fresh root ginger
100 g fig, plus extra to serve (optional)
1 orange, about 200 g
250 g carrot
100 g banana
ice cubes

1 Peel and roughly chop the ginger. Juice the fig and orange with the carrot and ginger.
2 Transfer the juice to a food processor or blender, add the banana and some ice cubes and process until smooth.
3 Pour the drink into a glass, add more ice cubes, decorate with sliced figs, if liked, and serve immediately.

makes about 200 ml

Recovery smoothie

2 kiwifruit, about 150 g
5 dried figs
300 ml almond milk
1 tablespoon protein powder
4 walnut halves
¼ teaspoon ground cinnamon

1 Peel and then juice the kiwifruit. Transfer the juice to a food processor or blender, add the remaining ingredients and process until smooth.
2 Pour the smoothie into glasses and serve immediately.

makes about 400ml

Fruit boost smoothie

150 g grapefruit
175 g pineapple
50 g kiwifruit
50 g frozen raspberries, plus extra to serve (optional)
50 g frozen cranberries

1 Peel and segment the grapefruit. Remove the skin and core from the pineapple. Peel the kiwifruit and juice with the grapefruit and pineapple.
2 Transfer the juice to a food processor or blender, add the frozen berries and process until smooth.
3 Pour the smoothie into a glass, decorate with raspberries, if liked, and serve immediately.

makes about 250 ml

Mean green juice

1 lemon
1 apple, about 125 g
1/3 cucumber, about 100 g
2 celery sticks, plus extra to serve
30 g kale
15 g parsley
ice cubes

1 Roughly peel the lemon and juice with the apple, cucumber, celery, kale and parsley.
2 Pour the juice into a glass over ice, add a trimmed celery stick and serve immediately.

makes about 450 ml

Broccoli & kale juice

100 g broccoli
100 g kale
50 g celery
25 g parsley
200 g apple
ice cubes

1 Trim the broccoli and kale. Trim the celery and cut it into 5 cm lengths. Juice the parsley and apple with the broccoli, kale and celery.
2 Pour the juice into a glass over ice and serve immediately.

makes about 200 ml

Specially for kids

Strawberries & custard smoothie

1 orange, about 200 g
1 mango, about 200 g
100 ml milk
60 g strawberries

1 Roughly peel and then juice the orange. Stone and peel the mango.
2 Transfer the orange juice and mango to a food processor or blender, add the milk and process until smooth. Pour the mixture into a glass.
3 Put the strawberries in the food processor or blender with 1 tablespoon of water and process until smooth.
4 Pour the strawberry mixture into the glass on top of the mango mixture. Stir a little to create swirls of the strawberry mixture in the smoothie. Serve immediately.

makes about 200 ml

Melon, carrot & ginger juice

250 g cantaloupe melon
1 lime
1 cm piece fresh root ginger
125 g carrot
ice cubes, to serve (optional)

1 Peel and deseed the melon and cut the flesh into cubes. Peel the lime. Peel and roughly chop the ginger. Juice the carrot with the melon, lime and ginger.
2 Pour the juice into a glass over ice, if using, and serve immediately.

makes about 200 ml

Strawberry, carrot & beetroot juice

250 g carrot
125 g beetroot
1 orange, about 200 g
125 g strawberries, plus extra to serve (optional)
ice cubes

1 Juice the carrot, beetroot and orange.
2 Hull the strawberries. Put the carrot, beetroot and orange juice in a food processor or blender, add the strawberries and a few ice cubes and process until smooth.
3 Pour the juice into a glass, decorate with a strawberry, if liked, and serve immediately.

makes about 300 ml
tip For a strawberry sunrise, hull 200 g strawberries and juice with 2 oranges – about 400 g in total. Pour into a glass, add some ice cubes and decorate with slices of strawberry.

Kiwifruit, melon & passionfruit juice

300 g watermelon
2 kiwifruit
200 ml passionfruit juice

1 Peel and deseed the melon and cut the flesh into cubes. Put the melon in a freezer container and freeze for at least 2 hours or overnight.
2 Peel and roughly chop the kiwifruit, then put them in a food processor or blender with the melon and passionfruit juice and process until thick.
3 Pour the juice into a glass and serve immediately.

makes about 300 ml

Mango, apple & cucumber slush

200 g apple
125 g cucumber
100 g mango
ice cubes

1 Peel the apple and cucumber. Peel the mango, remove the stone and roughly chop the flesh. Juice with the apples and cucumber.
2 Transfer the juice to a food processor or blender, add a couple of ice cubes and blend to make a fruity slush.
3 Serve immediately.

makes about 200 ml
tip For papaya, orange & cucumber juice, juice 125 g papaya flesh with the same amount of cucumber and 2 oranges.

Avocado & pear juice

75 g avocado
125 g pear

1 Peel the avocado and remove the stone.
2 Juice the pear and blend with the avocado.

makes about 150 ml
tip If you want to turn this into a tasty smoothie, triple the amount of pear you juice then whiz in a food processor or blender with a little ice.

Blackberry refresher

2 kiwifruit
100 g cantaloupe melon, cubed
100 g blackberries, plus extra to serve
100 ml apple juice

1 Peel the kiwifruit. Juice the melon, blackberries and kiwifruit, then put them in a food processor or blender with the apple juice and process with a couple of ice cubes.
2 Pour into a glass, decorate with a few extra blackberries and serve immediately.

makes about 200 ml

Orange, apple & pear juice

2 oranges, about 400 g in total
1 red apple, about 100 g
1 pear, about 225 g
ice cubes (optional)
1 teaspoon clear honey (optional)

1 Peel the oranges and divide the flesh into segments. Chop the apple and pear into even-sized pieces. Juice all the fruit.
2 Pour the juice into a glass over ice, if using, stir in the honey, if using, and serve immediately.

makes about 200 ml

Tomato, orange & celery juice

2 oranges, about 400 g in total
2 celery sticks, plus leafy stalks to serve
4 tomatoes, about 400 g in total
2 carrots, about 300 g in total
ice cubes

1 Peel the oranges. Trim the celery and cut it into 5 cm (2 inch) lengths. Juice the tomatoes and carrots with the oranges and celery.
2 Pour the juice into glasses over ice, decorate with leafy celery stalk stirrers and serve immediately.

makes about 400 ml

Apricot, nectarine & passionfruit juice

3 apricots, about 225 g in total
1 large nectarine or peach, about 125 g in total
2 passionfruit
150 ml apple juice
ice cubes

1 Cut the apricots in half and discard the stones.
2 Cut the nectarine or peach in half and discard the stone. (If your children don't like 'bits', peel the fruit before you start.)
3 Cut the passionfruit in half, scoop out the pulp and strain through a sieve to remove the seeds.
4 Put everything in a food processor or blender with a couple of ice cubes and whiz until smooth.
5 Pour into glasses and serve immediately.

makes about 400 ml

Banana & chocolate smoothie

1 banana, about 175 g
2 tablespoons organic cocoa powder,
 plus extra to serve
300 ml semi-skimmed milk
100 ml apple juice
2 large scoops vanilla ice cream

1 Peel and roughly chop the banana. Place in a food processor or blender with the cocoa powder, milk, apple juice and ice cream and process until smooth.
2 Pour into glasses, dust with cocoa powder and serve immediately.

makes about 400 ml

Mango, apple & blackcurrant smoothie

3 mangoes, about 600 g
2 tablespoons mango sorbet
100 ml apple juice
200 g blackcurrants or blueberries

1 Peel the mangoes, remove the stones and roughly chop the flesh. Purée the mangoes with the mango sorbet and half the apple juice. Set aside to chill.
2 Purée the blackcurrants with the rest of the apple juice.
3 Spoon the mango smoothie into glasses. Pour the blackberry purée slowly over the back of a spoon onto the mango smoothie. Drag a teaspoon or skewer down the inside of the glass, to make vertical stripes around the glass.

makes about 400 ml

Stripey berry smoothie

250 g raspberries
200 ml apple juice
200 g blueberries
4 tablespoons Greek yogurt
100 ml skimmed milk
1 tablespoon clear honey, or to taste
1 tablespoon wheatgerm (optional)

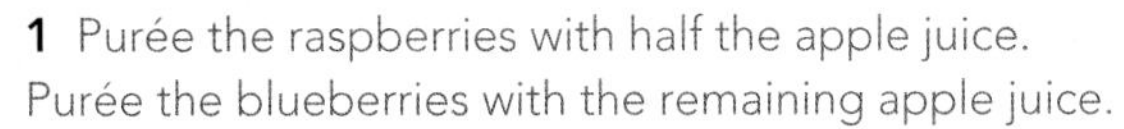

1 Purée the raspberries with half the apple juice. Purée the blueberries with the remaining apple juice.
2 Mix together the yogurt, milk, honey and wheatgerm, if using, and add a spoonful of the raspberry purée.
3 Pour the blueberry purée into a tall glass. Carefully pour over the yogurt mixture, and then pour the raspberry purée over the surface of the yogurt. Serve chilled.

makes about 200 ml

Berry cherry sparkler

150 g strawberries
125 g cherries
125 g watermelon
100 ml orange juice
500 ml sparkling water

1 Hull the strawberries. Halve and pit the cherries. Deseed the watermelon and cut it into small chunks.
2 Put all the fruit in a food processor or blender with the orange juice and blend until smooth. If your child will not like 'bits' in his or her drink, sieve the fruit purée over a bowl to remove the pips, skin and seeds.
3 Pour the purée into the glasses. Top up with the sparkling water.

makes about 600 ml

Traffic light smoothie

3 kiwifruit
150 ml lemon- or orange-flavoured yogurt
1 mango, about 200 g
2 tablespoons orange or apple juice
150 g raspberries
1–2 teaspoons clear honey

1 Peel and roughly chop the kiwifruit, then process in a food processor or blender until smooth. Spoon the purée into 2 tall glasses, and top each with a spoonful of yogurt, spreading the yogurt to the sides of the glasses.

2 Peel the mango, remove the stone and roughly chop the flesh. Blend the mango to a purée with the orange or apple juice and spoon it into the glasses on top of the kiwifruit purée and yogurt. Top with another layer of yogurt.

3 Blend the raspberries and push them through a sieve over a bowl to extract the seeds. Check their sweetness (you might need to stir in a little honey if they're very sharp) and spoon the raspberry purée into the glasses.

makes about 400 ml

Apple, peach & strawberry lollies

2 peaches, about 250 g in total
300 ml still water
1 red apple, about 100 g
125 g strawberries

1 Halve the peaches, remove the stones, roughly chop the flesh and juice.
2 Add one-third of the water and spoon the mixture into lolly moulds. Freeze until just set.
3 Roughly chop the apple and juice. Add one-third of the water and pour over the frozen peach mixture. Freeze until just set.
4 Hull the strawberries, then juice them. Add the remainder of the water, pour over the frozen apple mixture and freeze until set.

makes 3–4 lollies

Strawberry, mango & orange lollies

125 g strawberries
1 mango, about 200 g
300 ml orange juice

1 Hull the strawberries, then freeze them for 2 hours or overnight.
2 Peel the mango, remove the stone and roughly chop the flesh. Process the mango, frozen strawberries and orange juice in a food processor or blender until thick.
3 Pour the mixture into lolly moulds and freeze until set.

makes about 4 lollies

Glossary

agave nectar a commercial sweetener produced from several species of the agave plant.

avocado oil an edible oil pressed from the flesh of the avocado. It is used as a cooking ingredient in dishes and as a cooking oil.

almond milk can be made at home by grinding almonds with water or is available from supermarkets. It is darker than cow's milk and has a creamy texture and nutty taste.

alfalfa sprouts the shoots of the alfalfa plant, harvested before they grow into the mature plant. They contain concentrated amounts of some vitamins and minerals, such as vitamin C and calcium.

cinnamon dried inner bark of the shoots of the cinnamon tree. Available as a stick or ground.

cocoa nibs unprocessed cocoa beans, broken into small pieces. They have a chocolatey taste but are not as sweet as chocolate

cumin available both ground and as whole seeds; cumin has a warm, earthy, rather strong flavour.

dried fruit salad mix of dried prunes, apricots and apples available in health food stores. If you can't find it, substitute your own combination of dried fruits.

elderflower cordial a sweetened soft drink made from the flowers of the elderberry.

fromage frais a soft, unaged, creamy French cheese made from whole or skimmed milk and cream. Traditionally made with unpasteurised cream.

ginger, fresh also called green or root ginger; the thick gnarled root of a tropical plant. Can be kept, peeled, covered with dry sherry in a jar and refrigerated, or frozen in an airtight container.

goji berries the vibrant red fruit of *Lycium barbarum*. They have an intense flavour and contain valuable nutrients.

hot oat cereal a microwaveable mix of oats and oat flour, this is a form of instant porridge.

protein powders come in various forms – the most common being whey, soy and casein. They contain essential amino acids and are used as dietary supplements.

rosewater extract made from crushed rose petals; available from the baking aisle of supermarkets.

sesame seeds black and white are the most common of these tiny oval seeds; a good source of calcium.

soya milk a plant milk produced by soaking dried soyabeans and grinding them with water. Available from supermarkets.

turmeric a member of the ginger family, its root is dried and ground. It has an intensely pungent taste but is not hot.

vanilla pod dried long, thin pod from a tropical golden orchid; the minuscule black seeds found inside the pod are used to impart a distinctively sweet vanilla flavour to dishes.

wheatgerm the reproductive part of wheat that germinates to grow into a plant. Germ is a by-product of the milling process and is a rich source of vitamin E, B complex and protein.

Index

Conversion charts

liquids

METRIC	IMPERIAL
15 ml	½ fl oz
25 ml	1 fl oz
50 ml	2 fl oz
75 ml	3 fl oz
10 ml	3½ fl oz
125 ml	4 fl oz
150 ml	¼ pint
175 ml	6 fl oz
200 ml	7 fl oz
250 ml	8 fl oz
275 ml	9 fl oz
300 ml	½ pint
325 ml	11 fl oz
350 ml	12 fl oz
375 ml	13 fl oz
400 ml	14 fl oz
450 ml	¾ pint
475 ml	16 fl oz
500 ml	17 fl oz
575 ml	18 fl oz
600 ml	1 pint
750 ml	1¼ pints
900 ml	1½ pints
1 litre	1¾ pints
1.2 litres	2 pints
1.5 litres	2½ pints
1.8 litres	3 pints
2 litres	3½ pints
2.5 litres	4 pints
2.75 litres	5 pints
3.6 litres	6 pints

weights

METRIC	IMPERIAL
5 g	¼ oz
15 g	½ oz
20 g	¾ oz
25 g	1 oz
50 g	2 oz
65 g	2½ oz
75 g	3 oz
125 g	4 oz
150 g	5 oz
175 g	6 oz
200 g	7 oz
250 g	8 oz
275 g	9 oz
300 g	10 oz
325 g	11 oz
375 g	12 oz
400 g	13 oz
425 g	14 oz
450 g	14½ oz
475 g	15 oz
500 g	1 lb
625 g	1¼ lb
750 g	1½ lb
875 g	1¾ lb
1 kg	2 lb
1.25 kg	2½ lb
1.5 kg	3 lb
1.75 kg	3½ lb
2 kg	4 lb

teaspoons

DRY	
1 tsp	5 g
1 tbsp	15 g

LIQUID	
1 tsp	5 ml
1 tbsp	15 ml

PICTURE CREDITS

Dreamstime.com Pravit Kimtong 4. **Octopus Publishing Group** Vanessa Davies 14, 26, 110, 111, 112 left, 112 right, 114, 116, 117, 118, 119, 121; Janine Hosegood 31, 47; Lis Parsons 3, 13, 15, 16 left, 16 right, 17 left, 17 right, 18, 19, 21, 22, 23, 24 left, 24 right, 25 left, 25 right, 28, 29, 30, 32, 37, 38, 39, 40 left, 40 right, 41 left, 41 right, 42, 43, 44 left, 44 right, 45 left, 45 right, 48, 49, 50, 51, 52, 54, 55, 56, 57, 61, 62, 63, 64 left, 64 right, 65 left, 65 right, 66, 68, 71, 75, 76, 77, 78 left, 78 right, 79 left, 80, 81, 82, 84, 85, 89, 90, 91, 92 left, 92 right, 93 left, 93 right, 95, 96, 97, 98, 100, 101, 102 left, 102 right, 103 left, 103 right, 107, 108, 109, 113 left, 113 right, 122, 123; Gareth Sambidge 70, 79 right; William Shaw 67. **Shutterstock** Africa Studio 104; april70 99; Belinka 83 bg, 106; cluckva 6, 51 bg, 101 bg, 117 bg, 125 bg, 126 bg, 127 bg; designelements 60 bg; feiyuezhangjie 67 bg, 96 bg, 110 bg; Lukas Gojda 6; Alena Haurylik 10; Imageman 88 bg; Irsen.kh 33 bg; iulias 12; jannoon028 94; javarman 36 bg, 74 bg; Khristal 69; lola1960 9; Daria Minaeva 34, 46 bg, 58; Ortis 18 bg, 54 bg, 77 bg, 128 bg; Svetlana Prikhnenko 29 bg, 39 bg, 71 bg, 118 bg, 124 bg; Jane Rix 72; secondcorner 120 bg; somen 15 bg, 23 bg, 30 bg, 42 bg, 48 bg, 57, 62 bg, 80 bg, 85 bg, 90 bg, 109 bg, 123 bg; SongPixels 27; Sutichak Yachiangkham 20 bg; TGTGTG 86; vichkared 115; Welena 53 bg.